To Elaine M.L.

To Joanna and Lucy J.B.

Published by
The Dial Press
1 Dag Hammarskjold Plaza
New York, New York 10017

First published in Great Britain in 1981
by Methuen/Walker Books as *The Stickleback*

Library of Congress Cataloging in Publication Data
Lane, Margaret, 1907–   The fish.
Previously published as: The Stickleback. 1981.
Summary: Introduces the life cycle and mating habits of the small fishes
found in freshwater and saltwater in northern countries.
1. Three-spined stickleback—Juvenile literature.
[1. Three-spined stickleback. 2. Fishes] I. Butler, John, ill. II. Title.
QL638.G27L36 1982   597′.53   81-5545
ISBN 0-8037-2580-9   AACR2

THE FISH

The Story of the Stickleback

By Margaret Lane

Pictures by
John Butler

THE DIAL PRESS/New York

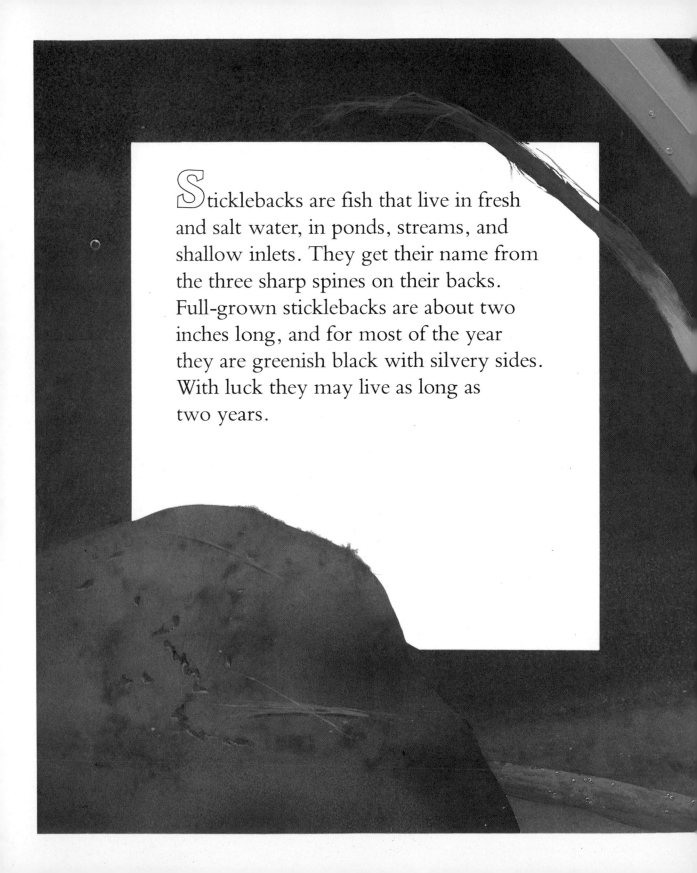

Sticklebacks are fish that live in fresh and salt water, in ponds, streams, and shallow inlets. They get their name from the three sharp spines on their backs. Full-grown sticklebacks are about two inches long, and for most of the year they are greenish black with silvery sides. With luck they may live as long as two years.

In spring, when the water begins to warm up and the days get longer, the male stickleback changes color. His throat and belly turn brilliant red, and his eyes become glittering blue. This will help him attract all the female sticklebacks who come near, but before they arrive, he must find a suitable place to build a nest.

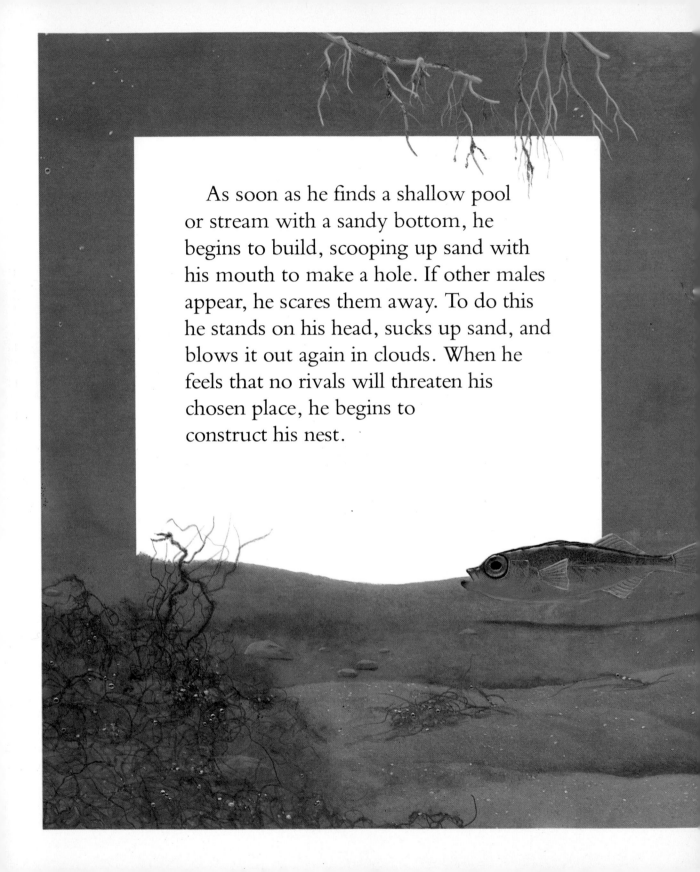

As soon as he finds a shallow pool or stream with a sandy bottom, he begins to build, scooping up sand with his mouth to make a hole. If other males appear, he scares them away. To do this he stands on his head, sucks up sand, and blows it out again in clouds. When he feels that no rivals will threaten his chosen place, he begins to construct his nest.

He bites off tiny weed stems and scraps of plants and binds them together with a fine sticky thread, much like a spider's, that he spins out from under his tail. When the nest is finished, it is like a soft tunnel anchored in the sandy hole. The stickleback fans the water with his fins, so that loose pieces of weeds float away from the nest.

If the first female to come near looks thin and plain, the male ignores her. But if she is fat and bulging with eggs, he becomes excited and darts around her in a zigzag pattern. This is his courtship dance. If the female is ready to lay her eggs, his bright color and fancy dancing will attract her. Her bulging shape is the thing that attracts him.

The male swims to the nest and hopes that she will follow. If she hovers near it, he pokes his head in to show her what to do. At last, after more dancing and urging, she slips into the nest while the male pushes her forward with his snout. The nest is soft and comfortable, and just the right size.

When the female is safely inside, the male touches her tail with his snout and moves in a vibrating rhythm. This movement starts her spawning, and a stream of jellylike eggs pours out into the nest. She may lay as many as a hundred, coming out of the nest thin and empty. The male, meanwhile, slips in and sprays his sperm all over the eggs. This makes the baby sticklebacks grow.

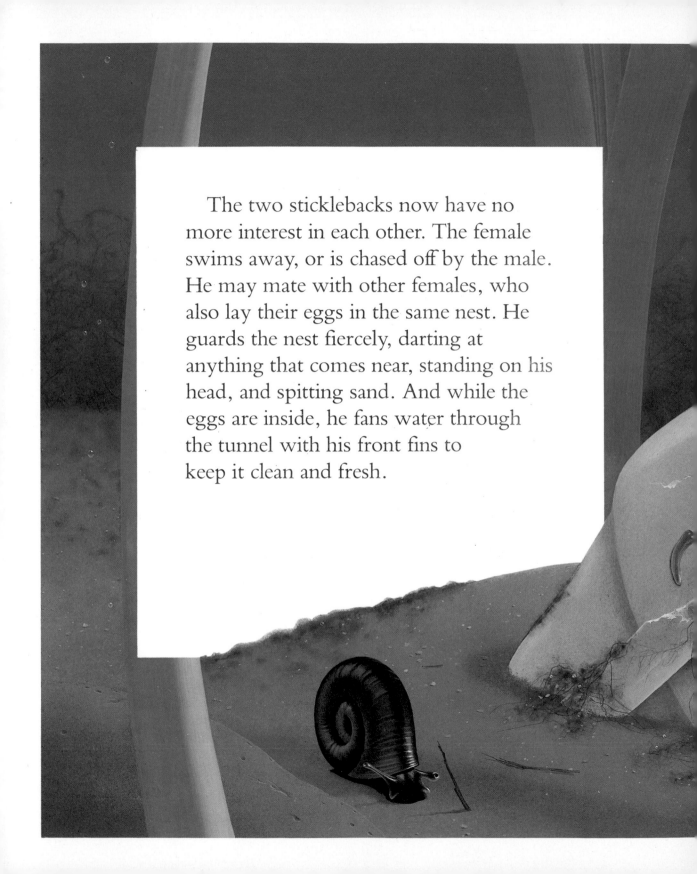

The two sticklebacks now have no more interest in each other. The female swims away, or is chased off by the male. He may mate with other females, who also lay their eggs in the same nest. He guards the nest fiercely, darting at anything that comes near, standing on his head, and spitting sand. And while the eggs are inside, he fans water through the tunnel with his front fins to keep it clean and fresh.

After five days black specks appear inside the eggs. These are the eyes of the baby sticklebacks. They are growing fast and already have hearts and tails. By about the ninth day they start to hatch, breaking out through the egg covering and hiding among the waterweeds. Still, the father keeps close to his family, attacking any creature that comes near.

If he did not guard them, few would survive. Young sticklebacks make a tasty meal for many hungry fish, birds, and other creatures. But when they are about two weeks old, the father stops caring for them and they have to take care of themselves, hunting water fleas and tiny worms. Meanwhile he will look for new mates and raise more broods. With luck he will have four or five families in a season.

When the last brood of the year is doing well, the male stickleback loses his bright color and is once more greenish black, like the female, with shadowy stripes on his back. Now bigger fish or birds will have difficulty spotting him and he is much safer from attack. The three sharp spines on his back are a good defense, too, making him painful to swallow.

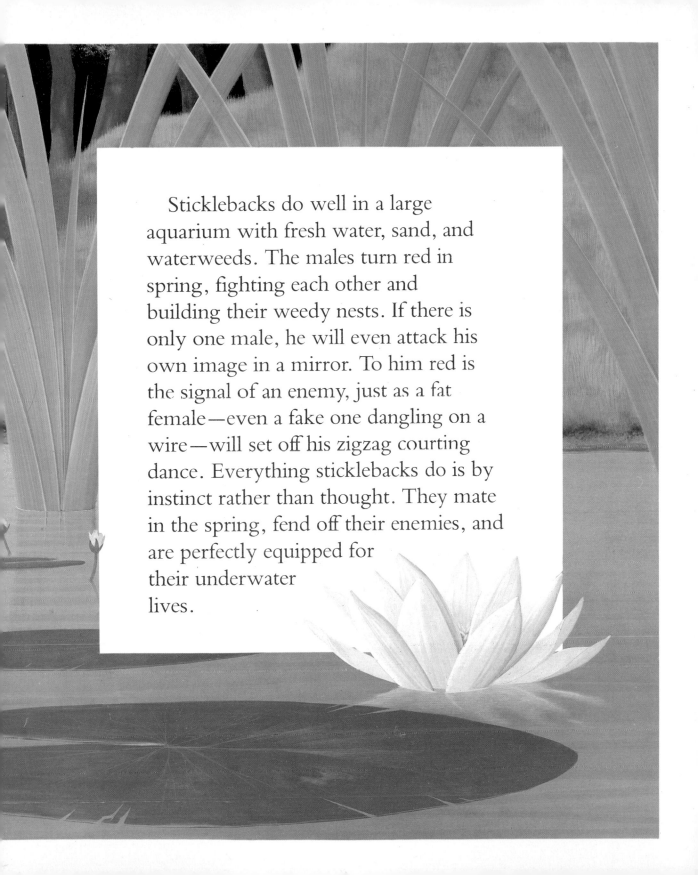

Sticklebacks do well in a large aquarium with fresh water, sand, and waterweeds. The males turn red in spring, fighting each other and building their weedy nests. If there is only one male, he will even attack his own image in a mirror. To him red is the signal of an enemy, just as a fat female—even a fake one dangling on a wire—will set off his zigzag courting dance. Everything sticklebacks do is by instinct rather than thought. They mate in the spring, fend off their enemies, and are perfectly equipped for their underwater lives.

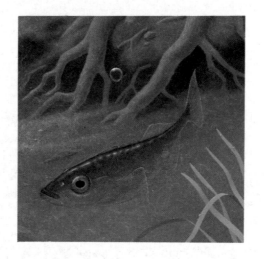